THE STORM BEHIND ME

a book of poems and pictures

Art by Sheri Wiseman and Poetry by Rory Piontkowski

The Storm Behind Me

To Jayla Ray – may you always chase your dreams

And Jaynee – for supporting mine

Rory Piontkowski

Alcohol ink on Canvas, 12 in. X 24 in.

The Storm

Rain falling, clouds thick,
Dark of twilight at noon.
Rare beauty of sky full of water,
Wind blows petulantly.

Boat tossed on the water,
Listless in the gale.
No direction, no control.
Short lived, but violent threat.

Drops pelt eyes and soak backs
Hunched against the force of Nature blowing.
Hope dashed against rock and reef,
Call for help lost in the howl.

Dreams crash like waves on the shore,
Time passes minutes like hours.
Remember this too shall pass
Seems like far away fables.

Fatih lost and faith-less,
Taking on water in the storm.
Overtakes faster than expelled,
Allies forgotten.

Am I lost?

Oil on Canvas, 24 in. X 24 in.

Sea of Night

I had a dream of sailing on the night,
It took me away for a while.
Today I wake up looking forward
Into the day, I smile.

My ship floats peacefully
Inside my bubble of light.
Outside the world grinds on
As I sail on a sea of night.

The seas' stars shine through deep water
Twinkling like the sun.
Flying on this wind behind me
I am the only one.

I find my peace here,
Life's cogs and keys turn outside.
There is beauty there also,
But I prefer here on the tide.

Sometimes the weight I can feel it
Pressing in from all sides.
It sits like a stone on my chest
Because on me it all rides.

I wonder where I am going,
Remembering where I have been.
What I have done and what I have said
All I can do is cringe.

In this, my light bubble,
All of that melts away.
I am at one with the elements
Often with nothing to say.

When I am ready I wake up
Ready to meet the day.
Eyes shining and tail bushy,
The stars of my sea light the way.

Oil on Canvas, 24 in. X 36 in

Coming up from the Dark

Tired of running and wary of none,
Up from the dark comes a leviathan.

The abuse and attacks,
Accepted until then,
Bring him up from the depths
From whence he was driven.

There will be no quarter given,
Or anger withheld.
The strike will come quick
With none left to tell.

No begging or pleading,
Nor praying or promise,
Will stop this behemoth
From moving beyond this.

Stormy sea, where they will all have to pay
At dusk when the sun's last light leaves the day.

Oil on Canvas, 18 in. X 24 in.

Unspun Sun Essence

An essence of sun,
sinfully,
Sits joyful and in play
There on her hair, it does.
I see her first
after moons have passed by.
I notice her again.

Unwound, undone,
unspun.
The sun lights where love falls.
Soft touch
Brings feelings' memory.

Time passes,
Space creeps in.
Hunger, need, survival.
Turning away.
Sun and moon mark time.

unspun essence of sun,
Moves across space,
filling time,
Closing feeling.
The last first
Brings it all back.
Together.

Oil on Canvas, 18 in. X 24 in.

Pier Fun

Tinkle of children's voices
And screams of half-fear
Carry over calm water
And through the night air.

Revealing an escape from time,
A revel of no-care.
An escape from the mind, a release from life's worries
At that pier with the fair.

Watching from afar I reflect,
Imagine the fun being had.
Melting away the days' trials,
Bringing clarity to the good and the bad.

Imagining the hundreds of smiles
On the faces of those having fun.
Children along with their parents
And young lovers wondering if this is the one.

No regret do I have, only memory,
Time's indifferent touch do I feel.
Wishing only that they have all the opportunity,
The choice to squander or make real.

Oil on Canvas, 36 in. X 48 in.

Moonrise

Calm, quiet,
Water lapping.

Orange orb,
Reflecting light.

Wait unbearable,
Once risen, accelerate.

Smaller as it rises,
Seems impossible.

Tiny boat more like a cork.
Rocks on waves leftover.

Smell of salt and feel of breeze.
Slow breaths.

Sea at night absorbs light,
Vastness rises up from the deep.

Perspective taken,
Worry melts away.

Oil on Canvas, 20 in. X 24 in.

ON THE EDGE

Life clings to certainty,
The rock of knowing and understanding.
Roots reach deep into crags of our humanity,
Like the connections between lovers and families.

Fear is like water in the cracks of a rock face
When the icy winds of winter start to blow.
When it freezes it begins to take up more space
And threatens to make cracks that show.

Once the cracks show, the damage is worsened
By the weight of what was once so strong.
So common to take what one person did, or said,
And let it become a picture of what we think is wrong.

Year after year of this process repeating,
Naturally anger replaces fear.
Anger eats away at the rock that's supporting,
Breaking connection with what was dear.

Only the strength of our convictions sound,
And that of those that love us,
Help keep us deeply rooted in the ground
When the cold fear becomes contagious.

Color alcohol ink on Canvas,
16 in. X 20 in.

WATER, COLOR

Light passing through water
Create color.

Life passing on daily
Create passion.

Time moving on quickly
Create space.

Be active.
Create.

Change your world.
Share with others.

Oil on Canvas, 18 in. X 24 in.

Wild Koi

Brother and sister,
Swimming together,
Twins from birth and forever.

Thoughts, one and the same,
They share swimming on through
The pond they were not born to.

Avoided as different,
They lean on each other
To stand up to all of the bother.

Until one day only one awoke,
The other had passed on.
Only the sister left, feeling sad and alone.

Knowing not what to think,
Or now how to manage,
Moving through her days feeling damaged.

One day another approached,
Asking if she would be open,
Saying he had been watching and hoping.

Needing a friend also, he said,
To share hopes and dreams with.
She was reluctant, nervous of possible grift.

The other kept up his pursuit
And over time her heart softened.
Not a replacement,
but one of whom she thought often.

No longer was she alone
Now celebrating life with the other,
But never forgetting her lost brother.

Oil on Canvas, 30 in. X 48 in.

Stormy Pagoda

Skies clear as the storm passes,
Clear blue and quiet remain.
Birds sing and the air is fresh.
Life resumes its flow again.

A world cleaned feels new,
This new beginning carries allure.
All is possible after the gale,
what was not thinkable before.

The breeze feels alive,
Carrying smells of wet flowers.
Drops glisten on grass and on buildings
Even after a few hours.

Time to get up and get out,
Try doing something new.
The storm brings clarity,
Opening up the world to you.

Oil on Canvas, 24 in. X 24 in.

KRAKEN

Safe and sound
On their hallowed ground
Their ancestors had worked so hard for.

Lifetimes ago
With shovel and hoe,
Building had been such a hard chore.

Children were born,
Crops were grown,
families enjoyed this modest existence.

Their beacon shown bright
Through the inky black night
Keeping ships safely at a distance.

But, as they all know,
Under the cliffs below
Moved an ancient danger.

A leviathan did creep,
Come up from the deep,
The unfortunate it did endanger.

When a child or man was lost
The village knew the cost
Was the sacrifice that must be exacted.

For the solitude they knew
They accepted that a lost few
Were worth the suffering extracted.

Oil and salt
on Canvas,
12 in. X 12 in.

The Storm Behind Me

The storm is behind me,
The cold and darkness lift.
Sun and clear skies welcome-
I made it.

I had not seen it coming,
But I suppose I knew it would.
When it came I felt prepared,
But I had forgotten what matters most.

How to appreciate,
How to love,
How to know who I was.
By those closest I am reminded.

A sense of relief,
Of understanding is here.
It fades as soon as I become aware,
Become comfortable.

The storm makes me afraid,
It challenges me.
I didn't ask for it,
But I welcome it.

SHERI WISEMAN,

mixed medium and oil painting artist.

I am a Utah based artist, creating unique art and scenic paintings full of texture and depth is my intention. I love to travel the world and I use the amazing things I've seen as the inspiration for my artwork.

You can find more of my artwork at sheriwisemanart.com.

RORY PIONTKOWSKI,

corporate road warrior moonlighting as poet and author.

After years of self-doubt, I finally decided to put down on the page for all what had previously only been in my head. I have been writing poetry for myself and those close to me for decades and have recently started writing a graphic novel.

Here's to finding your voice!

www.ingramcontent.com/pod-product-compliance
Lightning Source LLC
Chambersburg PA
CBRC100821120626
46547CB00010B/689